Coming of Age

Around the World

Anita Ganeri

raintree
a Capstone company — publishers for children

Raintree is an imprint of Capstone Global Library Limited, a company incorporated in England and Wales having its registered office at 7 Pilgrim Street, London EC4V 6LB – Registered company number: 6695582

www.raintree.co.uk
myorders@raintree.co.uk

Edited by Clare Lewis and Brenda Haugen
Designed by Richard Parker
Picture research by Gina Kammer
Production by Helen McCreath
Originated by Capstone Global Library Ltd
Printed and bound in China by CTPS

ISBN 978 1 406 29895 6 (hardback)
19 18 17 16 15
10 9 8 7 6 5 4 3 2 1

ISBN 978 1 406 29900 7 (paperback)
19 18 17 16
10 9 8 7 6 5 4 3 2 1

British Library Cataloguing in Publication Data
A full catalogue record for this book is available from the British Library.

Acknowledgements
We would like to thank the following for permission to reproduce photographs:
akg-images: Roland and Sabrina Michaud, 9; Alamy: © Anders Ryman, 17, © Chris Willson, 7, © Richard Levine, 11, © Tibor Bognar, 6; Capstone Press (map), throughout;
 Capstone Studio: Karon Dubke, 28, 29; Corbis, 16, © Penny Tweedie, 26, © Remi Benali, 21, © Tim Page, 10; Dreamstime: © Sebastian Czapnik, 23; Getty Images: Hyoung Chang, 14, LAWRENCE MIGDALE, 25, Niels Busch, 19, Nigel Pavitt, 13, Rob Melnychuk, 22; Glow Images/Corbis/© Hiya Images, 5; Newscom: Chameleons Eye/Rafael Ben-Ari, 24, DanitaDelimont.com Danita Delimont Photography/Brian McGilloway, 12, Eye Ubiquitous, 8, MCT/Chris Sweda, 15, Robert Harding Productions, 27, Robert Harding/Jane Sweeney, 20; Shutterstock: Christian Vinces, 18, violetblue, cover

We would like to thank Dr Suzanne Owen for her invaluable help in the preparation of this book.

Every effort has been made to contact copyright holders of material reproduced in this book. Any omissions will be rectified in subsequent printings if notice is given to the publisher.

All the internet addresses (URLs) given in this book were valid at the time of going to press. However, due to the dynamic nature of the internet, some addresses may have changed, or sites may have changed or ceased to exist since publication. While the author and publisher regret any inconvenience this may cause readers, no responsibility for any such changes can be accepted by either the author or the publisher.

Contents

Some words are shown in bold, **like this**. You can find out what they mean by looking in the glossary.

Growing up

In cultures around the world, important events in people's lives are marked with special customs and ceremonies. They help people to celebrate occasions, such as the birth of a baby, a wedding or to remember a person who has died. They are also a way of guiding people from one stage of their lives to the next. This book looks at how people from different cultures and religions celebrate "coming of age", when a child grows into an adult.

There are many different kinds of coming of age ceremonies. Some are challenges to prepare a young person for the responsibilities of being an adult. Some are religious celebrations that mark the change into an adult member of a faith. Others are big parties to celebrate this exciting new stage in life.

WHAT AGE?

When does a young person come of age? It depends where you live in the world. In some countries, 18 years old is the age when a young person officially becomes an adult. But in other places, there is no fixed age – it depends on a young person's experience and development.

In many countries and cultures, coming of age is a time for celebrating with a big party.

Coming of Age Day

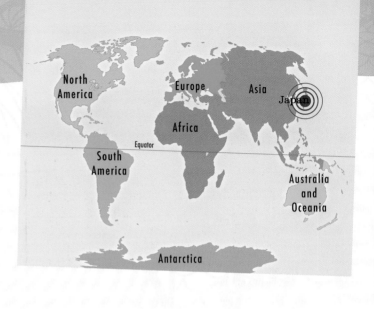

Every year in Japan, the second Monday of January is Coming of Age Day. This day is a national holiday to celebrate everyone who has reached their 20th birthday the year before. In Japan, the age of 20 is when a young person officially becomes an adult.

SPECIAL KIMONO

- For the Coming of Age Day celebrations, many young women follow ancient tradition and wear a special formal **kimono**, called a furisode. These beautiful kimonos are brightly coloured and made from silk. They are very expensive.

These young Japanese women are wearing beautiful furisode kimonos for Coming of Age Day.

Young men usually wear suits, but some choose to put on traditional dress, called the hakama.

Towns and cities all over Japan hold official ceremonies to mark Coming of Age Day. Every new adult is presented with a small gift. After the ceremonies, the young adults go to parties with their families and friends.

Old ways

Coming of age ceremonies are an ancient tradition in Japan. In the past, boys and girls were given their first adult clothes, and a new adult name. They also blackened their teeth and put on thick make-up as signs that they had become adults.

Sacred thread

When some **Hindu** boys are about 10 years old, a special ceremony is held to mark the end of childhood. It is called the Upanayana, or **sacred** thread ceremony. The day of the ceremony is decided by a priest. He studies a boy's **horoscope** to choose a lucky date. Then the boy's parents send out invitations to their family and friends.

A Hindu boy's sacred thread ceremony is a very important time in his life.

The ceremony can take place in the **mandir** or at home. First, the boy's head is shaved and he puts on new, clean clothes. Next, the sacred thread is sprinkled with water. Then, the priest puts the sacred thread over the boy's left shoulder and under his right arm. As he puts on the thread, the priest says the words of a Hindu prayer, the Gayatri Mantra.

FOUR STAGES OF LIFE

Traditionally, the life of a Hindu adult is divided into four stages. These stages are called ashramas:

1. **Brahmacharya** – life as a student
2. **Grihastha** – married and working life
3. **Vanaprastha** – retirement
4. **Sannyasa** – life as a wandering holy man (optional)

The boy wears the thread for the rest of his life. The ceremony marks the start of his adult life, and the beginning of his religious education.

Hindu ceremonies traditionally take place around a sacred fire.

The Five Ks

This young woman is welcomed into the Sikh faith during the amrit ceremony.

For young **Sikh** boys and girls, entering the Sikh Khalsa, or family, is an important part of growing up. An amrit ceremony is held in the **gurdwara** to welcome the young Sikhs into the Khalsa.

Before the ceremony, the boys and girls wash and put on clean clothes. They must wear the Five Ks (see box). The ceremony is led by five Sikhs who are already members of the Khalsa. They say special prayers while they prepare amrit, a mixture of sugar and water. During the ceremony, the boys and girls drink some of the amrit, and some is sprinkled on their eyes and hair. Afterwards, everyone shares a meal to show they are all equal.

These young Sikhs are wearing the Five Ks.

After the amrit ceremony, the young Sikhs are expected to live according to the rules of their religion.

THE FIVE KS

Kesh: uncut hair – shows devotion to God

Kanga: small wooden comb – a reminder of the importance of cleanliness and organization

Kara: steel bracelet – reminds Sikhs of their connection to God

Kirpan: sword – for protection

Kachera: cotton shorts – today worn as underwear (in the past they were more practical for everyday wear than the traditional long trousers worn in India)

Boy monks

In some **Buddhist** countries, such as Myanmar, boys leave home at the age of 10 to live as novice (trainee) **monks** for a few days or even years as part of their coming of age. In Myanmar, this important ceremony is called Shinbyu.

EAR-PIERCING

The novice monk is the centre of attention at Shinbyu. But his sister may also have a coming of age ceremony at the same time. Girls have their ears pierced and wear gold or silver earrings to show that they are now young women. They also wear beautiful dresses for the occasion.

This young boy in Myanmar is dressed as a prince, ready for his Shinbyu ceremony.

The boys ride to the ceremony on horseback, dressed in brightly coloured silk clothes. This is to follow the style of Siddhartha Gautama before he became the **Buddha**. He was a royal prince who gave up his life of luxury to become a monk. Before the ceremony, the monks shave the boys' heads. The boys promise to obey the 10 rules of behaviour for Buddhists. Then they put on simple **saffron**-coloured robes. The boys stay in the **monastery** to help the monks, and to learn more about the Buddha's teachings.

Novice monks in Myanmar wear traditional saffron robes. Some boys stay at the monastery and become monks for life.

Sweet fifteen

In Mexico and other Latin American countries, people celebrate a girl's 15th birthday as the time when she becomes a young woman. In these countries, the 15th birthday celebrations are called Quinceañera.

This girl is dressed for her Quincaeñera Mass.

In Mexico, the day begins with a **Mass** in church to welcome the girl to her new adult life. The girl wears a beautiful ballgown for the occasion. On her head she wears a tiara (small crown) to show that she is a princess, the daughter of God. She arrives at the church with her parents and **godparents**, and her "court of honour" made up of her brothers, sisters and friends.

It is traditional for the girl to wear flat shoes for her Quinceañera celebration. At the reception, her father gives her a pair of high-heeled shoes. The girl puts them on to show that she has left childhood and become an adult.

After the Mass, there is a party either at the girl's home or in a large hall. The girl makes a grand entrance. Then she dances with her father, and with her court of honour. There is a large cake, as well as dinner and speeches. The party goes on for hours!

Dancing is an important part of a girl's Quincaeñera celebrations.

Sunrise dance

In the United States, the Apache Native Americans hold a four-day coming of age ceremony for girls. It is called the Sunrise Ceremony. It is a great test of **stamina**, as the girls must dance for hours at a time.

Each girl is led through the ceremony by a godmother and a medicine man. The godmother dances with the girl and helps her throughout the ceremony.

Dancing for hours on end is seen as a test of the girl's strength and character.

CHANGING WOMAN

According to Apache myth, the very first woman is called Changing Woman. She gives birth to twin boys, Monster Slayer and Child Born of Water, who save the Apache people from terrible monsters. When she grows old, Changing Woman walks east towards the sun until she meets her young self coming back. In this way, she is born again and again, generation after generation.

The godmother remains a special person for the rest of the girl's life. The medicine man leads the ceremony.

During the four days of the ceremony, the girl must not wash herself or touch her own skin. She drinks only through a special tube. She must run, dance and sing. The Apache believe that these ceremonies celebrate the myth of Changing Woman, and that they help the girl grow into a strong woman.

As part of the ceremony, the girl is painted with a white pollen mixture.

Coming of age challenges Around the World

In many places, boys and girls must face tough challenges before they are allowed to enter the adult community. The aim of these challenges is to prepare them for adult life.

Stinging ants

The Satere Mawe tribe live in the Amazon rainforest in Brazil. Boys of this tribe go through a very painful challenge to prove they are ready to become men. They put on special gloves that are filled with stinging bullet ants. The boys try to wear the gloves for 10 minutes but it is very difficult. The effects of the ant stings last for hours after the gloves come off. The boys must do this 20 times before they become adults.

The bullet ant has an extremely painful bite.

Fire-jumping

The Ticuna tribe also live in the Brazilian rainforest. To prepare them for their lives as young women and mothers, girls from this tribe spend up to six months alone. Afterwards, there is a four-day ceremony, when the girls must jump over fire, dance and sing without any sleep.

Adult warriors of the Maasai tribe often wear colourful clothes.

Warriors in training

Maasai boys from Kenya and Tanzania in East Africa face many challenges as they become adults. To prove that they are ready to become warriors, they put on black clothes and paint their faces white. Then they are sent to live apart from their village in a camp built by their mothers. They stay there for 4 to 8 months, looking after themselves.

Jumping the cattle

The Hamar tribe in Ethiopia make their living as cattle herders. Young men of this tribe take part in a difficult "cattle jumping" coming of age ceremony. Once the ceremony is complete, the young men are allowed to own cattle, get married and have children.

These young Hamar tribesman are getting ready for the cattle jumping ceremony.

A Hamar man must run across the backs of the cattle, without falling off.

The coming of age ceremony lasts for three days. There is feasting and drinking before the day of the cattle jumping. To prepare for the jumping, a young man is rubbed with sand to wash away all his badness. Then, around 15 cattle are lined up side-by-side. They are covered with dung to make them slippery. Each young man must run and jump across the backs of all the cattle. If he falls, he can try again. He must do this four times before he can become an adult member of the community.

A HELPING HAND

Even if a young man is disabled or blind, he can still take part in the cattle jumping ceremony. Friends and family will lift him over the backs of the cattle, or he can run under the necks of the cattle.

Confirming your faith

Anglicans can take part in the Communion service once they have been confirmed.

For **Anglican Christians**, confirmation is a special service for young people to confirm their beliefs and promise to follow the teachings of Jesus Christ. Confirmation means "making something firmer or stronger". In this service, the young people are confirming the promises that were made by their parents and **godparents** at their **baptism**, to bring them up as Christians. But now they are old enough to understand these beliefs and promises for themselves.

First Communion

Young people often go to confirmation classes before the service, to learn about their faith and the promises they are making. During the service, they are welcomed

as full members of the Christian Church. Then they take **Holy Communion** for the first time. During Communion, each person takes a small piece of bread and a sip of wine. For Anglican Christians, the bread represents Jesus's body and the wine represents his blood. In this way, Christians give thanks for Jesus's life and death.

These young Christian boys and girls are dressed up for their First Communion.

Bar and Bat Mitzvah

In the **Jewish** religion, boys and girls have a special ceremony to mark the start of their adult religious life. For boys, it is called Bar Mitzvah, and it takes place after their 13th birthday. Bar Mitzvah means "a son of the commandment". A Jewish girl can become Bat Mitzvah ("a daughter of the commandment") after her 12th birthday.

A Jewish boy reads from the Torah at his Bar Mitzvah.

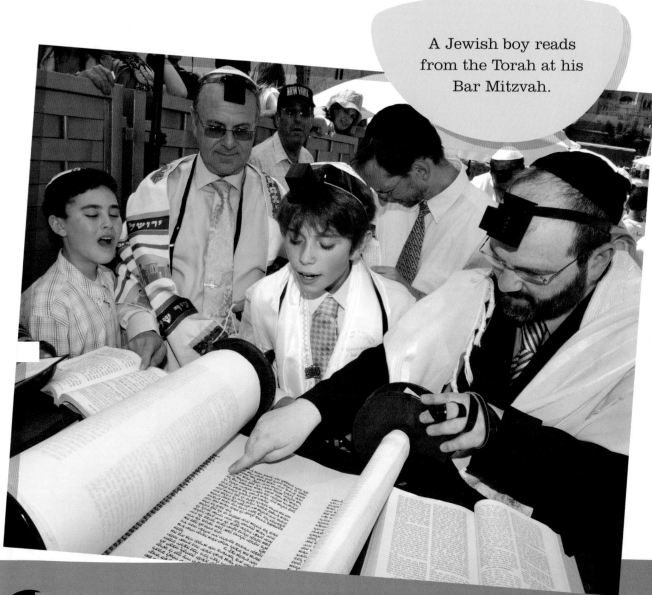

Bar Mitzvah

Boys must study hard before their Bar Mitzvah ceremony. They have to learn the **Hebrew** language so that they can read from the **Torah**, the Jewish holy book. They also go to special classes in the **synagogue** to study their religion. The ceremony takes place in the synagogue. The boy reads a passage from the Torah. Then he is blessed by the **rabbi**. After the service there is a party. The boy is given gifts and good wishes by all of his family and friends.

BAT MITZVAH

In some synagogues, a girl's Bat Mitzvah service is the same as a boy's Bar Mitzvah. The girl is welcomed as a full member of her synagogue, and of the Jewish community.

This girl is taking part in her Bat Mitzvah ceremony in the synagogue.

Going on walkabout

The Aboriginal people have lived in Australia for tens of thousands of years. For the Aboriginals, walkabout is an important tradition that links them to their ancient **ancestors**.

When some Aboriginal boys are around 12 or 13 years old, they go on walkabout for about six months. They leave their homes and families and go into the bush, the dry, hot middle part of Australia. They must look after themselves, build their own shelter and find their own food and water. Before they leave, their families teach them some of the skills that they will need to survive.

This young Aboriginal boy is about to go on walkabout.

Dreamtime

The Aboriginal people believe in the Dreamtime, a time of creation when the land, humans and animals were formed. The boys learn about the land, and about the paths trodden by their ancestors. When they return to their families, they are ready for their adult responsibilities.

ANCESTOR SPIRITS

Dreamtime stories have been passed down from generation to generation. The Aboriginal people believe that "ancestor spirits" gave the land, plants and animals their form. The power of the ancestor spirits is still everywhere in the Australian landscape.

Paint a **walkabout pebble** picture

As Aboriginal children grow up, they learn about their culture through stories (see page 27). The stories are often told through paintings. Go on a walkabout in your local area, and create your own dot painting.

1 Ask an adult to tell you stories about your local area. Go on a "walkabout" together and find a large pebble, shell or piece of wood to decorate. Give it a coat of black or brown paint, and leave it to dry.

2 Choose bright colours to make a pattern. Dip a stick (or the end of a paintbrush handle) into the first colour. Dot the paint onto the pebble.

3 Keep adding dots in the same colour to build up a wavy line or shape.

4 Choose a new colour. Add another line of dots, following the shape of the first line.

5 Keep building your picture using different colours. Find objects to make dots of different sizes (try the ends of a pencil, the points of a fork or the tip of a cocktail stick).

6 Leave your pebble to dry overnight.

Your dot painting could show special animals or plants from your local area.

7 When the paint is completely dry, brush it with watered-down PVA glue. This will protect your design and stop the paint from chipping off.

Glossary

ancestor relative from the past

Anglican Christian member of the Anglican group of Christians

baptism when a person takes part in a ceremony to become a full member of the Christian Church

Buddha Buddha is the title given to the man whose teachings Buddhists follow

Buddhist person who follows the religion of Buddhism

godparent person who promises to help bring up a child as a good Christian

gurdwara Sikh place of worship

Hebrew language in which the Jewish holy books are written

Hindu person who follows the Hindu religion

Holy Communion ceremony in which Christians share bread and wine to remember Jesus

horoscope chart showing the position of the stars and planets at the time of a baby's birth

Jewish connected with the religion of Judaism. A Jew is a person who follows Judaism.

kimono traditional Japanese silk dress

mandir Hindu place of worship, sometimes called a temple

Mass service held in some Christian churches

monastery building where monks live

monk man who devotes himself to his religion

rabbi Jewish religious teacher

sacred special, usually to do with religion

saffron yellow-orange colour

Sikh person who follows the Sikh religion

stamina strength over a long time

synagogue Jewish place of worship

Torah part of the Jewish scriptures

Find out more

Books

Around the World in 500 Festivals, Steve Davey (Kuperard, 2013)

Encyclopedia of World Religions (Internet-linked Encyclopedias),
   Susan Meredith (Usborne, 2010)

What Do You Believe? Aled Jones (Dorling Kindersley, 2011)

Websites

www.bbc.co.uk/nature/humanplanetexplorer

This brilliant website has stunning photos and video clips showing how people live around the world. There is a section on life events, including birth, childhood, coming of age, finding a partner and death.

www.bbc.co.uk/religion/religions

Find out more about the world's religions on this fact-packed website. There is also an interfaith calendar which looks at celebrations and holy days in different cultures.

Further research

Which of the ceremonies or rituals in this book did you find most interesting? Can you find out more about one of them? For example, you could find out more about the Five Ks in the Sikh coming of age ceremony. You can look in books, on the internet, or ask your friends.

Index